# LEE

Edited by

## NEIL JEFFRIES

CARLTON
BOOKS

First published by Carlton Books 2002

A CIP catalogue record for this book is available from the British Library.

ISBN 1 84222 735 1

Printed in Singapore
1 3 5 7 9 10 2 4 6 8

# INTRODUCTION

From Don Revie to the likes of Billy Bremner, Norman Hunter and even Eric Cantona, those associated with Leeds United have never been short of a good one-liner, or even a *bon mot*!

So if you want to know why Olivier Dacourt thinks Eddie Gray is like Forest Gump, or how scary Gordon Strachan's feet are, or what Lucas Radebe thinks of his good friend Mr Mandela, then you'll find out in this small, but perfectly formed, collection of quotes.

**❝**I'm hard but fair – like
Leeds United.**❞**

**Mr Mackay** *to Fletcher in* Porridge *pilot*
*'Prisoner And Escort'*

" They had the all-white kit modelled on Real Madrid. They looked like a team of ghosts. No wonder they never lost. "

**'Mad' Frankie Fraser**

"I used to love Leeds United. They were all geniuses. But I had to put football aside when I got into shoes."

**Vic Reeves**

"It was a very proud moment when I raised the FA Cup above my head. No other Leeds captain had done that before."

**Billy Bremner**

❛When Billy Bremner received the FA Cup off the Queen, he never handed it to the rest of us. I asked him why not. He said, "Allan, I'd waited long enough to get my hands on that, I wasn't going to pass it down to you lot!"❜

**Allan Clarke**

'This place is for the haves
and the have yachts'

**John Lukic** *visiting Monte Carlo for the UEFA Cup tie
against AS Monaco*

❝ He may have had a bit of a weight problem. He liked his food and a beer now and again. But he was one of the great guys. One that you'd want to be in the trenches with. ❞

**Lee Chapman** *on Mel Sterland*

'Ever since I was a kid all I
wanted to do was play
in midfield.'

**Rio Ferdinand**, *Leeds and England
central defender*

*On the pitch, when I see green or smell green, I get a little bit crazy. The grass, you know? I get this green mist.*

**Jimmy Floyd Hasselbaink**

"He transfixed the static Liverpool defence like a stoat on the rabbit."

**Stewart Hall** *on Jimmy Floyd Hasselbaink in 1998*

❝ The peak of Jimmy Armfield's ambition was to manage Blackpool, his home-town club, and play the organ in his local church. It actually took him six months to decide whether he wanted to manage the reigning Champions. I came up with the immortal phrase, "The manager's indecision is final", and it was perfectly true. ❞

**Duncan McKenzie**

❝Awful, I used to hate it. He was only 28 and he looked about 40. I didn't like kissing him goodnight when he had that on his face.❞

**Gabby Logan** (*née Yorath*) *on her father Terry's moustache*

" Ereek, 'ow does it feel to bee scooring yor fust goal for Leeds? "

**Lee Chapman** *'translates'* Yorkshire Television's
John Helm's question to new French signing
*Eric Cantona*

‟I want Leeds to be able to match them on all counts; to have won everything in sight; to be a magnetic drawing card wherever we play… in fact, I want us to be better than anyone else.”

**Don Revie** *before seeing his side beat Manchester United 1–0 at Old Trafford on 30 October 1971*

**❝**John Charles was the best
header of a ball I've seen. And
when he played that ball was
solid. Now, with the ball as it is,
he could probably head it about
100 yards – further than
I could kick it.**❞**

**Denis Law**

**❝**I'll get in trouble with my girlfriend if I play – I don't think she'll be too happy if I'm chasing Totti all over Rome.**❞**

**Jonathan Woodgate** *on his chances of making only his second start for Leeds, away to AS Roma in the UEFA Cup in 1998*

**❝**This referee's so poor, I'd
have been booked just getting
off the coach.**❞**

**Norman Hunter** *watching Mike Reed in 1998*

"A snarling angry Alsatian was literally inches away from my thigh before the police handler grabbed his head an pulled him away. As I ran on I shouted over my shoulder, "I only crossed the ball – it's Lee Chapman you want, he's the one that put your team down.""

**Chris Kamara** *on the post match pitch invasion after Leeds won promotion at Bournemouth in 1990, simultaneously relegating their hosts*

❝ I did hear the bang but I didn't realise at first what had happened. Then I just felt this burning pain and my left leg went numb. The car started to skid, and I put my hand down to my side and I could feel the blood. ❞

**Lucas Radebe** *on the moment he realised he'd been shot while driving through his native Soweto*

"If teams knew Ian Baird was playing, it wasn't shin-pads they reached for, it was gum-shields."

**Ian Snodin**

❝To say that Leeds are playing with Southampton is the understatement of the season. Poor Southampton, they just don't know what day it is. The Leeds side are just turning it on. Ah! Look at that… it's almost cruel.❞

**Barry Davies** *commentating on Leeds 7 Southampton 0 on 4 March 1972*

❝He is told there is so much money to buy one good player. So he goes out and buys David Batty and then utilises the rest, the best of which cost nothing and are barely old enough to drink.❞

**Jimmy Greaves** *on David O'Leary becoming Leeds manager in 1998*

**❛**Go on, take yourself off to the Kop.**❜**

**Don Revie** *at Anfield, encouraging his team –
which had just clinched the 1970 League
Championship by holding their hosts and nearest
rivals to a 0–0 draw – to approach the biggest and
most fearsome set of fans in Britain*

# ❝Champions! Champions! Champions!❞

**The Liverpool Kop** *salutes Revie's Leeds players on 28 April 1969*

❝Music from the Victor Sylvester Dance Orchestra echoed across the pitch from the tannoy and we were ordered by the major to take our partners… The dancing was supposed to improve our rhythm and make us play like Brazilians. It didn't – we just fell about and he scrapped the idea in favour of hypnotism.❞

**John Charles** *on the unorthodox training methods employed by manager 'Major' Frank Buckley*

This young man... has already proved he possesses the ability, temperament and wisdom which makes a good young player into a truly great one.

**Billy Wright**, *captain of England, writing of John Charles in 1951*

"I knew Paul Madeley, Paul Reaney, Norman and Clarkey from the England set-up, and the others I'd played against numerous times. I've still got the bruises to prove it. "

**Tony Currie** *on fitting into the rebuilding Leeds side after his move from Sheffield United in 1976*

'I got on with Jimmy Adamson. He was a strange fellow, though. He had Dave Merrington as his number two, and he was a total nutcase, too.'

**Tony Currie**

❝We were robbed… definitely robbed – at the last gasp. And just after our valiant-hearted lads had run themselves into the ground. My God, did you see their faces? They were drained. I hadn't seen expressions like that since Dunkerque.❞

**Rigsby a.k.a. Leonard Rossiter** *recalls*
*Leeds' controversial defeat in the 1975 European Cup Final*
*in an episode of* Rising Damp *later that year (script by*
*Eric Chappell)*

‘We were a better side than Bayern Munich. We weren't beaten by a better side. We were beaten by a bad referee.’

**Jimmy Armfield** *manager of the Leeds side that lost the 1975 European Cup Final 2–0 to Bayern Munich in controversial circumstances in Paris*

❝ I was always singing – at training sessions, in my room, in the canteen. The lads were always saying to me, "You should be in Boyzone rather than a footballer." ❞

**Nicky Byrne** *one-time Leeds United youth team 'keeper who left to join Westlife*

**❝**He harpooned me! And after I had driven 300 miles, to be there, too. The challenge was so late that I had a dig at him about it. Norman just laughed and said he got there as quick as he could.**❞**

**Kevin Keegan** *on playing against Norman Hunter in his 1975 testimonial (Leeds versus Revie's XI – virtually the full England side)*

**❝** I was never any good
at friendlies. **❞**

**Norman Hunter**

❝I've never been superstitious, although I've played with a lot of people who have been. When I played for Leeds, it was all I could do to find a place in the line I could walk out in. They all had their particular places and I just tried to shuffle in.❞

**Eddie Gray**

❝In my early days at Leeds, when there were international games on, there'd be just me and Mick Bates left behind for training.❞

**Trevor Cherry**

'I think, given a second chance, he'd have come in and been a bit more diplomatic.'

**Trevor Cherry** *on Brian Clough*

❝Without doubt the best Leeds striker I played against was Allan Clarke. He was a special talent and you knew you were in for a difficult time. He was a handful to mark and, putting it diplomatically, he could always look after himself.❞

**David O'Leary** *on his time as an Arsenal defender against Leeds*

**❝**I didn't enjoy playing against Leeds. There was no honour in their football. I never got the impression that they were enjoying themselves. They were sour, winning was all, and they were paranoid about criticism.**❞**

**Bobby Charlton** *on the team that his brother Jack enjoyed playing for so much*

❝When thirty-odd thousand stood up and applauded me, making it clear I was their choice to take over, it was a very moving moment and a memory I'll cherish.❞

**David O'Leary** *recalling how the fans' vote, as he walked to the dugout (as caretaker manager) for the match against Martin O'Neill's Leicester (3 October 1998) persuaded him to take the manager's job if offered it*

‘Harry Kewell – he's Australian
and anyone with a bit of
Australian in them will do.’

**Nasser Hussain** *names a Leeds player he'd like
to play cricket for him*

**❛**Leeds, Leeds Reserves, Leeds youth teams, Leeds Permanent Building Society pub team, Leeds & Holbeck pub team, Leeds ice hockey team, East Leeds chess under-19s, South Leeds over-75s poker team, anyone else with Leeds in their name. And Middlesbrough.**❜**

**Jonathan Woodgate** *on whose results he looks for first*

"We always had a bottle of Scotch in the dressing room – me and Bobby Collins used to like a little sip before we went out."

**Peter Lorimer**

**❛** Don Revie used to say that football is all about players, and that was his philosophy throughout the time that I knew him. Everything he did was with that in mind, he looked after us and our families superbly well. **❜**

**Paul Madeley**

"I used to give him the ball and say, "When you're bored with that TC, you can give it me back". He had such great skills."

**Norman Hunter** *on Terry Cooper*

‘Even now I have to pinch myself about playing here. When I was young I could never have dreamed of it.’

**Lucas Radebe**

" Lucas would come to training with one leg and apologise for not giving 100 per cent. My life would be a lot easier with a team of Lucases. "

**David O'Leary** *on Lucas Radebe*

People use the word "great"
far too easily, but Billy really was
a great player.

**Norman Hunter**

' Billy always thought Leeds were his club and rightly so – he was Leeds through and through. Nothing gave him greater pride than pulling on that Leeds United shirt. When he had that badge on his chest, it was then he was proudest. '

**Eddie Gray**

He picked the ball up near the corner flag and you just ran out of counting the number of times he went past defenders. He beat Tommy Docherty's son Michael about three times. It was 20 seconds before anyone realised he'd put it in the back of the net. Everyone was dumbfounded.

**Billy Bremner** *on Eddie Gray's second goal at Elland Road in the 2–1 in over Burnley, 4 April 1970*

"For a man so small in size, he's a person of great stature who can destroy the big guys with one lash of his coruscating tongue."

**Howard Wilkinson** *on Gordon Strachan*

**❝**I actually got more pleasure out of the first one in that game, it was a more measured goal.**❞**

**Eddie Gray** *on his first-half chip from the edge of the Kop end penalty area*

"He was so crafty that he would just seem to disappear. Then from nowhere, the ball was in the net and who scored? Allan Clarke!"

**Billy Bremner**

❛The secret to our success was that we played to a system and we knew instinctively how we were going to play it, People just played better than they should have done.❜

**Lee Chapman** *on the 1992 Championship*

**❛**It has to be viewed over a three-year period – to go on from that initial platform to win the title must rank as the most telling testimony to a team's character there has ever been. **❜**

**Howard Wilkinson** *on the 1992 Championship*

Side before self –
every time.

**Billy Bremner**

"I've never been one for regrets or hard luck stories, but we dominated the game from start to finish – and Munich know that more than anyone."

**Billy Bremner** *of Bayern's controversial 2–0 defeat of Leeds in the 1975 European Cup Final*

**❝**I have worked with some truly influential players in the past but never one to match the part Gordon Strachan played in my career or in the development of Leeds.**❞**

**Howard Wilkinson**

"Norman bites yer legs.

*Banner carried by* **Leeds fans** *circa 1972*

> **"** I tell you, there were far tougher lads than me around in the league. **"**

**Norman Hunter**

"He had a will to win I have never seen in any player I have come across before or since. He would play a game – snooker, table tennis, anything – for eight hours if need be, until he won a game."

**Terry Cooper** *on Norman Hunter*

‘Keep your hair short, your clothes smart and don't get caught up with loose girls.’

**Don Revie** *advising his squad on discipline*

"Technically, he was absolutely outstanding, but perhaps temperamentally, it's fair to say he wasn't the best in the world. He did drop some terrible clangers in big games."

**David Harvey** *on Gary Sprake, the goalkeeper he eventually replaced*

**❝**Careless hands…**❞**

**The Liverpool Kop** *singing to Sprake after the Leeds man threw the ball into his own net at Anfield*

"We were meant to report for training at ten o'clock, but you could guarantee that most or all of the players were there for half-past-nine, just for the craic."

**David Harvey**

❝I had an exam that week, so I could either go with the lads (parading the 1992 Championship trophy round the streets of Leeds in an open-top bus) or stay home to revise. I decided to work. Looking back I think, "What the hell was I doing?"❞

**David Wetherall** *BSc (Hons) Chemistry*

"Why I love you, I don't know why I love you, but I love you."

**Eric Cantona's** *message to the Leeds fans from the balcony of the Town Hall in 1992, which was eventually immortalised in song*

❝To keep learning, all the time, is probably one of the most important things. If you ever stop learning, then how are you going to improve yourself?❞

**Harry Kewell**

❛I'm not worried about anyone.
I'd rather play against the
world's best defence.
I don't care.❜

**Harry Kewell** *aims high*

❝ We're all going potty in the stands, in the commentary position. Injury time Leeds 4 Derby 3… and they were 3–0 down. ❞

**Bryn Law** for BBC Radio Leeds breathlessly summarises the greatest Leeds comeback in living memory, 8 November 1997

**❝**I like Jimmy but I wouldn't go
on the dole for him.**❞**

**David O'Leary** *on reports that he said he'd quit if*
*Jimmy Floyd Hasselbaink was sold*

❝If we were a goal down, he would automatically go up front and try to create things. And if it broke down, he'd be tearing back into defence. He was just that type of player, such a great footballer.❞

**Mick Jones** *on Billy Bremner*

❛You could say I am really the number one captain among a team of captains when I step out with Leeds.❜

**Billy Bremner**

❝You never count the ones
when you got beat.❞

**John Sheridan** *dismisses all the great goals
scored when Leeds didn't win*

‘I always dress from the left –
left shinpad, left sock, left boot.
It's stupid but I've always
done it. ’

**Paul Robinson**

❝When I kicked a ball I didn't have to think about rhythm or power. It was natural ability, an automatic action, and a gift for which I will always be grateful.❞

**Peter Lorimer**

# ❛ Nine-ty miles an hou-r! ❜

**Leeds supporters'** *chant from the 1970s*
*saluting Lorimer's measured shooting speed*

**'** There's no way you could win
it better **'**

**Don Revie** *to Brian Clough on YTV's* Calendar
1974 *after Clough, recently sacked by Leeds,
declared it had been his ambition to improve on the
way Revie's team had won the title in 1973–74*

❝I can't imagine him jumping for the ball. One of his false eyelashes might come out.❞

**George Graham** *on Tomas Brolin, the multi-million misfit he inherited from Howard Wilkinson in 1998*

**‘** He said just two words to me
in six months – you're fired! **’**

**Tomas Brolin** *on George Graham*

'Clarke… one–nil!'

**David Coleman** *commentating on the 1972
Centenary Cup Final – and a catch phrase at many,
many other games in the 1970s*

❝In terms of physicality, the
Leeds team of the '70s was the
best I've ever seen.❞

**Michael Parkinson** *rues the passing of the
old-fashioned 'man's game' in 1999*

'You cannot put into words Tony Yeboah's ability in front of goal. The players and the management have all been amazed and surprised at the quality he has shown.'

**Howard Wilkinson**

"I love to score the beautiful goals."

**Tony Yeboah**, *scorer of so many*

"It was as if Nora Batty was going to be the evening's entertainment and Pamela Anderson turned up instead."

**Frank Wiechula** of the Daily Mirror on the Leeds fans' reactions to seeing their side come from 3–0 down to beat Derby 4–3, Premiership, 8 November 1997

**❝**I want to get it
choreographed, like
Busby Berkeley. **❞**

**Paul Trevillion**, *marketing genius, pitches
synchronised warm-ups – along with sock tabs,
target balls, personalised tracksuits etc –
to Don Revie in 1970*

❝With England sometimes I've been away for a week preparing for 90 minutes of football. I could turn up at five to three and play a game.❞

**David Batty** *and his no-nonsense approach to football*

‘ Gary Kelly is the maddest one
at Leeds United. Without
prompting he was climbing
head first into wheelie bins. ’

**Paul Robinson** *on the 1999 Leeds United*
*Christmas outing*

**"** I do it at home, as well, strolling around like Tarzan in just a pair of Nikes. The neighbours know me pretty well. **"**

**Gary Kelly** *on team-mates' reports that he irons in the nude even when sharing a hotel room at away matches*

❛When we got to Paul Madeley, whoever was doing the introductions said, "This is Big Ed." I suspected the lads were trying to trick me into calling him Bighead. But you couldn't have met anyone less arrogant. Later I found out it really was his nickname; Edward was his middle name.❜

**Brian Flynn** *recalls meeting his team-mates for the first time in 1977*

**❛**My toes are like horrible wee bits and bobs. It scares people on the beach as I walk along in my thong.**❜**

**Gordon Strachan** *on the long-term effects of having his toenails pulled out by the roots to avoid discomfort as a player*

" Anybody who tells you they are happy with their squad is lacking in ambition. We will always look to improve it. "

**Peter Ridsdale** *in 2000*

**❝**I'd have Peter Ridsdale as Mr. Big – silver hair, a big chair and a fat cigar, masterminding it all – like the Nöel Coward role in *The Italian Job*. **❞**

**Hugo Speer**, *star of* The Full Monty, *plays casting director*

"You look around and think, if we could go down, with so much talent, then God must always be with you."

**Lucas Radebe** *talking about plane crashes rather than relegation after an emergency landing at Stanstead airport on the way home from a game with West Ham, 28 March 1998*

**❝**With England he didn't have
the players he had available
at Leeds.**❞**

**Johnny Giles** *suggests the spell as national team*
*manager taught Don Revie he had been spoilt at*
*club level*

❝ Just two defeats in 42 games shows a tremendous consistency of effort, attitude and work. ❞

**Johnny Giles** *reflects on the 1969 Championship win with some degree of understatement*

Some kids aspire to be pilots, doctors or cricketers. I had only one vision, there was no Plan B – it had to be soccer.

**Harry Kewell**

❝Harry had a very determined attitude from the day he arrived. He was always convinced that he was going to be a footballer. It wasn't a case of if, but when, as far as he was concerned.❞

**Eddie Gray** *on Kewell's burning ambition evident from the day he joined as a 16-year-old trainee in 1995*

'The lifestyle is much the same
– bad clothing, bad food – so
we don't expect too much. '

**Alfie Haaland** *on why Norwegians such as he
and Eirik Bakke can settle so well in England*

" It flew into the top corner but it could just as easily have hit the corner flag. "

**Terry Cooper** *recalls his goal that beat Arsenal 1–0 at Wembley and won Leeds their first major trophy – the League Cup of 1968*

'It was an absolute privilege to have played with the two greatest left-sided centre-backs in football: Bobby Moore and Norman Hunter.'

**Terry Cooper** *on his team-mates at England and Leeds respectively (though in Hunter's case they played together at both international and club level)*

❛Norman had this reputation of being an animal on the football park – but off it he was a complete gentleman.❜

**Billy Bremner** *on Norman Hunter*

" I was worst when we were getting beat. I've got to be honest, at times I used to get the red mist and the head used to totally and utterly go. "

**Norman Hunter**

*I hadn't been able to spot trouble brewing in the past and steam-rollered straight into it. Howard Wilkinson taught me how to see when the troubles were coming.*

**Vinnie Jones**

"Leeds were the team I never wanted to leave."

**Vinnie Jones** *at Elland Road for just two seasons, 1989–91*

❝Vinnie Jones was no card player. We used to love having him around – by God did me and Imre Varadi take him for a few quid!❞

**Mel Sterland** *on the big loser in The Big Hitters card school*

"I can never ever remember Don Revie telling us to go out and kick anybody. All he used to say to me was, "Norman, let them know you're there – first tackle!"

**Norman Hunter**

I don't think I'd be as hard as Norman but certainly if it came to the real deadly stuff then I would be more dangerous.

**Johnny Giles**

"I think really and truly people disliked us at Leeds. But we didn't mind. In fact, it probably made us the team we were."

**Norman Hunter**

‘ He's very fit, very fit for his age... unbelievable. He is Forrest Gump! ’

**Olivier Dacourt** *on Eddie Gray*

**❝** Regardless of what people say about skill and natural ability, if you can't run you can't play. **❞**

**Eddie Gray**, *still fit enough to train the first team squad, in 2000*

'He didn't talk to anybody in the reserves. Howard was so focused on what the first team was doing that if you weren't in the team, you didn't exist.'

**John McClelland** *on Howard Wilkinson*

"I wanted Eric to stay but he did what he'd done all through his career. Manchester United were the only club that offered us the million pounds back that we had spent on Eric. People thought we were a rich club back then, but a million pounds was still a massive amount to Leeds."

**Howard Wilkinson** *on why Eric Cantona was sold to Leeds United's biggest rivals in 1992*

❝ Norman was a great tackler, one of the best tacklers you ever saw. But on the odd occasion, he'd miss-time one. ❞

**Jack Charlton**, *not known as a man who ever took prisoners*

"I had a good memory of people who'd done nasty things to me. I'd get them back if I had the chance but I would do it within the laws of the game when the ball was there. I was a good tackler – you can tackle as hard as you like."

**Jack Charlton** *denies he ever really had players on his hit list*

**❛**It was a classic goal.
George Weah might bend it
round the wall and curve it into
the net but when you score lying
on your back facing the wrong
direction, people will never
forget it! **❜**

**Lucas Radebe** *on his overhead strike in
the UEFA Cup against Partizan Belgrade, 14
September 1999*

"First of all there's the
Boss who's right behind us,
He's the one who fills our hearts
with pride."

**Les Reed** - *the first two lines of 'Leeds Leeds
Leeds' the A-side of the 1972 Leeds United single*

"I would not be bothered if we lost every game as long as we won the League."

**Mark Viduka**

**❝** First team, first team give us a song. **❞**

*6,000 **Leeds fans** locked in the San Siro sing to the first team squad sat on the grass in front of them after the Champions League 1–1 draw with AC Milan on 8 November 2000*

**❝**The best bit of player-fan
bonding I have ever seen.**❞**

**Alan Green** *on BBC Radio 5 Live describing the
Leeds squad singing back*

" After losing my front teeth there was nothing holding me back. "

**Joe Jordan** *explains his fearless approach to playing centre-forward*

"In my eyes, no one's worth
that kind of money. How can you
be worth millions and millions
of pounds?"

**Rio Ferdinand** *on his own record-breaking*
*£18-million price tag*

❛It's all part and parcel of the modern game, but somehow I can't imagine Jack Charlton and Johnny Giles in such a tender embrace.❜

*Comedian* **Ardal O'Hanlon** *considers the sight of Gary Kelly kissing Stephen McPhail as part of a goal celebration*

❛Leeds play well… very
aggressive, physically. The
attackers are incredible. They
come pressing you from all over,
don't let you have time
to breathe.❜

**Paolo Maldini**, *legendary Italian defender, on
David O'Leary's Leeds*

❝ Relegation was, without doubt, the worst thing that's happened to me in football. Leeds were my team: for them to drop out of the top division was a disaster. I was in tears. It was a nightmare time, a stigma we'll always have. ❞

**Terry Connor**, *the Leeds-born striker, looks back in anguish at the end of the 1981–82 season*

'We were frightened
of nobody. Everybody was
frightened of us – it
was lovely!'

**Jack Charlton**

❝I was a great fan of Don Revie. I admired him so much because he didn't want to leave any stone unturned. He was a meticulous planner.❞

**Kevin Keegan** *on the dossiers on opponents that Revie developed at Leeds and took with him to the England job*

❝My one regret is that I didn't let you lads off the leash earlier. When it mattered most I was too cautious.❞

**Don Revie**, *to Johnny Giles, shortly before his death on 26 May 1989*

**❝**Mr Mandela is in fantastic shape for someone who is 82 years old – he moves faster than me!**❞**

**Lucas Radebe** *during an official visit to Leeds by his friend, the former South African president, in April 2001*

**❝** You get nowt for
being second. **❞**

**Billy Bremner** *on his general will to win. It was
also the title of his 1969 autobiography*

‘ People didn't give us enough credit for picking it up every time. After what we'd been through, a lot of clubs, a lot of players, would have collapsed. ,

**Johnny Giles**

‘If it was there to be won,
I would try to win it. In fact, even
if it wasn't there, I'd still try.’

**Kenny Burns**

❛I got knocked out by Kenny Burns, after two minutes. The ball was out for a throw-in and he looked around, to make sure no one was watching, and just punched me.❜

**Mark Lawrenson** *the ex-Liverpool player and now TV commentator*

❝I am quite a gruesome person. I did have a scrapbook on the Yorkshire Ripper… That was one of my most treasured possessions.❞

**David Batty**

"I don't want you to take this personally gaffer, but if I'm not back in the team, you might find yourself sleeping with the fishes."

**Vinnie Jones**, *brandishing a double-barrelled shot gun, to Howard Wilkinson*

❝The neighbours on one side have got a villa in Portugal, the other side have got a house in America. We're looking for one in Filey.❞

**David Batty**, *a man of simple tastes*

In my mind I never play a good game. I know I can do better. If I scored ten goals in a game I'd want 11.

**Harry Kewell**

❝They said, "We've got to get four doctors. We need two to pull your arm that way, and two more to pull it the other way." And that's when I threw up.❞

**Mick Jones** *recalls the moment in the dressing room when the shock of dislocating his arm at the 1972 Centenary FA Cup Final finally hit him*

**❝** Jimmy could really hit a ball.
Jimmy could sidefoot a ball as
hard as most people could
strike it. **❞**

**Nigel Martyn** *on his former team-mate*
*Jimmy Floyd Hasselbaink*

❝I take a size eight but I used to have a seven-and-a-half in a boot. And I always wore two pairs of socks. I like a snug fit.❞

**Allan Clarke**

I've seen myself referred to as "a legend". I've been called worse, let's put it that way.

**Robbie Fowler**

**❝**Leeds are going mad and
they have every right to.**❞**

**Barry Davies** *commenting for the BBC on
protests from players and fans following referee Ray
Tinkler allowing a clearly offside West Brom goal that
cost Leeds the 1971 League Championship*

'Leeds? I hated them... but I loved to hate them. I didn't respect them, I feared them, because they were a great team.'

**Ian McCulloch** *of Echo And The Bunnymen, a Liverpool fan, on Don Revie's team*

"We had the babies looking after the young babies."

**David O'Leary** *on drafting in a few reserves to the team that beat Portsmouth 5–1 in the FA Cup in 1999*

❝The changing rooms are full of under-17-year-olds, tiny lads in Leeds training gear – there's loads of them.❞

**Stephen McPhail** *on the next generation of "Leeds babies" at the Thorp Arch training ground*

'Once people left Manchester United, everyone used to think you went away, curled up and died... I didn't fancy that, dying a death at 32.'

**Gordon Strachan** *on leaving Manchester United and joining Leeds United*

❝The kids came through from the swimming pool and said that Leeds had signed Vinnie Jones. I started laughing and they said no, it was serious. I leapt into the pool, but thought, "There's no point in drowning yourself, you're getting well paid."❞

**Gordon Strachan***'s thoughts when he heard Vinnie Jones was joining the club*

'There's more chance of us signing Father Christmas than Robbie Fowler.'

*Leeds United Chairman* **Peter Ridsdale** *in December 2000 on the possibility of signing the striker*

❝I didn't think I deserved the vote, it is supposed to be for the worst trainer of the week. I wasn't even there for most of it as I was with the Republic of Ireland. I only trained last Friday and I wasn't bad on that day.❞

**Ian Harte** *on receiving the Robin Reliant awarded to the worst team member in training during the week who then had to drive it to the ground on the next match day*

❝You need a bit of luck in these situations. Every time I had a sniff of a goal it went in.❞

**Mark Viduka** *modestly explains how he scored all four goals when Leeds beat Liverpool 4-3 at Elland Road on 4 November 2000*

He has got one thing that Allan Clarke had and that is a nasty streak. That is absolutely essential for any striker.

**Paul Hart** *on Alan Smith*

"His temperament is sometimes very hot, but I don't think you should avoid playing him because of that."

**Sven-Göran Eriksson** *on Alan Smith*

❝Lock that boy up in a cage and throw away the key until he's a Leeds player. Don't let any other club near him.❞

**Jack Charlton** *on Eddie Gray in 1964 after the teenaged Gray had run rings round him in a trialists' match*

❝You could run a university course on how to score goals based on Robbie.❞

**David O'Leary** *considers Robbie Fowler excellent value for £11 million*

**❝**He's played with swollen
ankles, with pulls, with colds,
with his legs black and blue.
He's turned out with knocks,
with strains, with cuts. So
determined is Norman that never
once has he said he is unfit.**❞**

**Don Revie** *speaking of Norman Hunter's allegiance
to the game and the club*

"No manager could wish for a greater leader or a greater player. If I was in the trenches at the front line, the man I would want at my right-hand side is Billy Bremner."

**Don Revie** *speaking of Billy Bremner in 1974*

'Every time Leeds concede a goal I feel like I've been stabbed in the heart.'

**Billy Bremner**